U0497960

孔子学院总部 /
国家汉办汉语国际推广成都基地规划教材

走 进 天 府 系 列 教 材【成都印象】

居成都

Living in Chengdu

西 南 财 经 大 学
汉语国际推广成都基地　著

西南财经大学出版社
中国·成都

西 南 财 经 大 学
汉语国际推广成都基地 著

总策划 涂文涛

策 划
李永强

主 编
梁 婷 白巧燕

编 者
《成都印象·游成都》 胡倩琳
《成都印象·居成都》 郑 莹
《成都印象·吃川菜》 谢 娟 王 新
《成都印象·品川茶》 肖 静
《成都印象·饮川酒》 谢 娟
《成都印象·看川剧》 郑 莹
《成都印象·绣蜀绣》 谢 娟
《成都印象·梦三国之蜀国》 蒋林益 胡佩迦
《成都印象·悟道教》 沙 莎 吕 彦 陈 茉
《成都印象·练武术》 邓 帆 刘 亚

审 订 冯卫东

英文翻译
Alexander Demmelhuber

Introduction

Living in Chengdu is one part of the "Impressions of Chengdu" textbook series, which is promoted by the Chengdu Base of Confucius Institute Headquarters and published by the Southwestern University of Finance and Economics. This book contains 6 units, which are designed on the basis of the Confucius Institute Headquarters'/Hanban's "International Curriculum for Chinese Language Education"(hereinafter referred to as "Curriculum"), as can be seen, for example, on vocabulary and language points used, and ensures that this textbook is held to scientific, systematic and rigorous standards.

This book portrays life in Chengdu: it gives an overview about Chengdu, transportation, foreign cuisine, leisure life and work. The lessons strive to be as practical as possible, vivid and colorful, and aim to help international students of Chinese learn about life in Chengdu through language and background information.

This book is mainly composed of vocabulary and grammar items as can be found in the Curriculum for levels 2 to 4, with some everyday Chinese expressions mixed in. We hope that this book will help beginner students of Chinese to lay a solid foundation for their Chinese and comprehensively improve their proficiency.

Hopefully, you will enjoy *Living in Chengdu* and we are looking forward to any criticism or suggestions you might have. Hanban gave us much help and support during editing of this book and we would like to take this opportunity to express our gratitude.

前言

　　《居成都》是西南财经大学汉语国际推广成都基地推出的"成都印象"系列教材之一。全书共6课，以孔子学院总部/国家汉办的《国际汉语教学通用课程大纲》为基本编写依据，涉及大纲中的大量词汇、语言点等指标，以保证教材的科学性、系统性和严谨性。本书以在成都居住和生活为线索，介绍了成都的基本情况、交通、外国美食、休闲生活、工作等内容，力求贴近生活，为外国汉语学习者在成都生活提供语言和信息的支持。本书语言材料以大纲中的2—4级词汇和语法项目为主，加入了一些生活中的常用汉语，希望能够为初级水平的汉语学习者打下扎实的基础，全面提升汉语水平。

　　希望您能喜欢《居成都》这本教材，也希望您对本书提出批评和建议。本书的编写得到了国家汉办的大力支持和帮助，在此一并表示感谢。

目录

第一课
Lesson 1

【西部中心城市：成都】
【The Western Central City: Chengdu】

① 经 济　jīngjì
② 交 通　jiāotōng
③ 中 心　zhōngxīn
④ 历 史　lìshǐ
⑤ 便 利　biànli
⑥ 气 候　qìhòu
⑦ 舒 适　shūshì
⑧ 热 情　rèqíng

　　成都在中国的西南部，是四川省的省会。成都是中国西部经济和交通中心，也是历史文化名城和中国最佳旅游城市之一。这里交通便利，气候舒适，人们快乐热情。年轻人喜欢住在成都，因为这里的工作环境好，机会多；老年人喜欢住在成都，因为这里的生活很舒服，有美食、有美景……

文小西：
　　大萌，我在机场看见一句话"成都，一座来了就不想离开的城市"。为什么这么说？

大　萌：
　　你刚到成都不久，还不太清楚。

江一华：

我觉得一定是因为成都有很多吸引人的地方，所以人们不想离开。

大萌：

对，那你们觉得成都有哪些方面吸引人呢？

文小西：

首先应该是气候吧，我可不喜欢太热或者太冷的地方。

大萌：

成都的气候不冷也不热，年平均温度16℃。气候非常适合居住。

文小西：

成都有太多好吃的东西了，我每天都能发现新的小吃，我的胃每天也都好满足！

大萌：

是的，川菜很好吃，而且在全世界都很有名。

江一华：

我觉得成都最大的优点是房价和消费不高，生活节奏比较慢，我不会觉得太紧张。每个人都很享受生活，周末和朋友喝茶、聊天、打麻将，日子过得特别舒服。

① 吸　引　xīyǐn
② 平　均　píngjūn
③ 温　度　wēndù
④ 小　吃　xiǎochī
⑤ 胃　　　wèi
⑥ 满　足　mǎnzú
⑦ 优　点　yōudiǎn
⑧ 房　价　fángjià
⑨ 消　费　xiāofèi
⑩ 节　奏　jiézòu
⑪ 享　受　xiǎngshòu
⑫ 麻　将　májiàng
⑬ 常　常　chángcháng
⑭ 感　觉　gǎnjué
⑮ 幸　福　xìngfú

大 萌：

　成都阴天比较多，所以阳光是这个城市最大的礼物。有阳光的周末，许多人就会放下学习和工作，和家长、朋友出去玩，尽情享受阳光。

文小西：

　在这里我常常感觉心情很好，越来越觉得离不开成都了，想一直住在这里！

大 萌：

　成都是2017年中国最有幸福感的城市，很多人来了就不想离开。

Chengdu is in the southwest of China and is the capital of Sichuan Province. Chengdu is the center of economy and transport in western China and is a city of history and culture. It is also China's best tourist city. Here, transport is good, the climate is comfortable, and the people are happy and warm-hearted. Young people like to live in Chengdu, because the working environment here is good, with opportunities abound; the elderly like Chengdu, because life here moves at a slow, comfortable pace, and there are also the good food and the nice sceneries…

Wen Xiaoxi: Da Meng, at the airport, I saw this phrase, "Chengdu: once you've arrived, you'll never want to leave." Is that true?

Da Meng: You haven't been here for long; you wouldn't know.

Jiang Yihua: I think that's because Chengdu has a lot of attractive places, so people don't want to leave.

Da Meng: Right! What do you think makes Chengdu appealing?

Wen Xiaoxi: First off, the climate. I don't really like overly hot or overly cold places.

Da Meng: Chengdu's climate is moderate, and the average annual temperature is 16°C, which makes the city a perfectly suitable place to live.

Wen Xiaoxi: Chengdu also has so many tasty foods! Every day I'm discovering new snacks to eat. My belly can't complain!

Da Meng: True, Sichuan food is tasty and also known throughout the world.

Jiang Yihua: I think that Chengdu's biggest plus are its low living and housing costs. I don't feel stressed thanks to the slow-paced living. Everybody enjoys life and has a really good time, like drinking tea, chatting or playing mahjong with their friends on weekends.

Da Meng: Chengdu has a lot of cloudy days. Sunshine is this city's biggest gift. On sunny weekends, a lot of people will put aside study and work to go out and enjoy the sun.

Wen Xiaoxi: I'm often in a good mood here. I feel more and more attached to Chengdu. I want to stay here forever!

Da Meng: In 2017, Chengdu was named China's happiest city. A lot of people who come here don't want to leave.

词 语

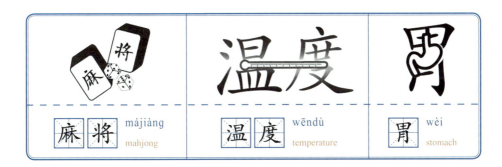

麻 将 májiàng mahjong	温 度 wēndù temperature	胃 wèi stomach

xī yǐn 吸 引	attract; draw; fascinate	píng jūn 平 均	average
xiǎo chī 小 吃	snack	mǎn zú 满 足	satisfied; content
yōu diǎn 优 点	merit; strong point	fáng jià 房 价	cost of housing; house pricing
xiāo fèi 消 费	consumption; expenditure	jié zòu 节 奏	pace; rhythm; tempo
xiǎng shòu 享 受	enjoy	shěng huì 省 会	capital

cháng cháng 常 常	often; frequently		gǎn jué 感 觉	feel
xīn qíng 心 情	mood; frame (or state) of mind		xìng fú 幸 福	happy; happiness
zhōng xīn 中 心	center; heart; core		jīng jì 经 济	economy
jiāo tōng 交 通	traffic; transportation		biàn lì 便 利	easy; convenient
lì shǐ 历 史	history		qì hòu 气 候	climate
shū shì 舒 适	cosy; snug; comfortable		rè qíng 热 情	passionate; enthusiastic

思 考

1. 你以前到过成都吗？你觉得成都怎么样？

2. 读课文，说说成都有哪些吸引人的地方。

3. 读课文，说说成都人怎么过周末。

第二课
Lesson 2
【宜居的成都】
【Chengdu: A Livable City】

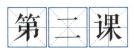

（一）

① 内 地　nèidì
② 宜 居　yíjū
③ 最 近　zuìjìn
④ 环　　huán
⑤ 高架桥　gāojiàqiáo
⑥ 广 场　guǎngchǎng
⑦ 日 常　rìcháng
⑧ 休 闲　xiūxián
⑨ 锻 炼　duànliàn
⑩ 增 加　zēngjiā
⑪ 乐 趣　lèqù
⑫ 晒　　shài
⑬ 散 步　sànbù
⑭ 发 呆　fādāi

大萌：

一华、小西，你们来看看这篇文章：《成都被评为中国内地最宜居城市》。

江一华：

最近我也慢慢感受到了成都的宜居，这里干净美丽。我特别喜欢二环路高架桥下的绿色植物，觉得很有新意。路边有很多公园，每天都有老年人在公园里跳舞。

大萌：

那是"广场舞"，是中老年人日常休闲生活的一部分。广场舞让他们既见了朋友，又锻炼了身体，还增加了生活的乐趣。

江一华：

对，我也常常看到有人在公园里晒太阳、聊天、散步。成都不仅茶馆多，咖啡馆也多。有一次我在路上看到一家可爱的咖啡馆，走进去，里面是轻柔的音乐、美味的咖啡、安静的人们……我爱上了成都这样美好的生活。

大 萌：

　　是的，咖啡馆也是人们常去的地方。一个人去咖啡馆点杯咖啡，看书、发呆，一坐就是一下午。或者约朋友一起去喝喝咖啡，聊聊天，时间过得很快。

（二）

① 中　介　　zhōngjiè
② 房　租　　fángzū
③ 根　据　　gēnjù
④ 合　同　　hétóng
⑤ 方　便　　fāngbiàn
⑥ 红旗连锁　Hóngqí Liánsuǒ
⑦ 舞东风　　Wǔ Dōngfēng
⑧ 食　品　　shípǐn
⑨ 日用品　　rìyòngpǐn
⑩ 中国电信
　 Zhōngguó Diànxìn
⑪ 中国移动
　 Zhōngguó Yídòng

江一华：

大萌，我最近想搬到学校附近住，我该怎样找房子呢？

大萌：

你最好去找个房屋中介，中介费一般是一个月的房租。他们会根据你的要求带你去看房子，看好了房子以后要跟房东、中介一起签合同。

江一华：

住在学校附近方便吗？

大萌：

学校附近有大商场和超市，比如麦德龙、西单商场，也有很多小商店，非常方便。成都差不多每条路上都有"红旗连锁"和"舞东风"超市，可以买食品和日用品，也可以充公交卡、交水电气费，甚至买旅游的车票。学校离地铁口也很近，可以到四号线的西南财大站、七号线的文化宫站坐地铁。旁边还有金沙公交站，交通非常方便。

江一华：

　我先去中介公司问问。还有一个问题，我想在家上网，这个麻烦吗？

大　萌：

　你可以去中国电信、中国移动等公司问问，它们的工作人员会去你家给你安装网络。

（三）

文小西：

　一华，我妈妈想给我寄点东西，但是我不知道学校的地址。你知道吗？

江一华：

　成都市青羊区光华村街55号。

文小西：

　青羊区？为什么叫这个名字呢？

大　萌：

　因为青羊宫在这个区，所以叫青羊区。

① 寄　　　　jì
② 区　　　　qū
③ 青羊宫　　Qīngyáng Gōng
④ 听说　　　tīngshuō
⑤ 道教　　　Dàojiào
⑥ 建筑　　　jiànzhù
⑦ 摸　　　　mō
⑧ 关系　　　guānxì
⑨ 琴台路　　Qíntái Lù
⑩ 抚琴小区　Fǔqín Xiǎoqū
⑪ 文学家　　wénxuéjiā
⑫ 小子　　　xiǎozi
⑬ 表达　　　biǎodá
⑭ 汇合　　　huìhé
⑮ 合江亭　　Héjiāng Tíng
⑯ 浪漫　　　làngmàn
⑰ 锦官驿街　Jǐnguānyì jiē
⑱ 街道　　　jiēdào
⑲ 想象　　　xiǎngxiàng
⑳ 气息　　　qìxī

江一华：

我听说青羊宫是一座很有名的道教建筑。

大萌：

是的，青羊宫里面有两只青羊，传说摸青羊宫的青羊会有好运。

江一华：

我发现成都很多地名都和历史有关系。

大萌：

对，比如现在的琴台路和抚琴小区，都跟司马相如和卓文君的故事有关。司马相如是汉代的文学家，那时他是个穷小子，卓文君是富人家的女儿，司马相如抚琴来表达爱意，之后两人追求爱情来到成都生活。

文小西：

这么看，成都也是个有爱的城市。

大萌：

说得好。另外还有一个地方叫合江亭。成都的母亲河是府河和南河，两条河合在一起叫府南河。1 200 年前，人们在两条河汇合的地方修了合江亭。现在很多年轻人在结婚的那天早上，也会去合江亭拍照。

文小西：

两个人开始在一起生活，像府河和南河的汇合，真浪漫！

江一华：

我知道有条街叫锦官驿街，是因为成都古时候被称作"锦官城"。

大萌：

是的，成都的街道名有很多故事。

文小西：

想象那些街道曾经发生过很多历史故事，而现在仍然充满了生活气息。真是太有趣了！

Part 1

Da Meng: Yihua, Xiaoxi, come here and look at this article: "Chengdu named most livable city in inland China".

Wen Xiaoxi: These days, I have also gradually experienced Chengdu as a livable, clean and beautiful place. I really like the green plants under the viaduct of the second ring road. What a nice idea! There are many parks on the roadside. Every day, the elderly dance in the parks.

Da Meng: That would be "square dancing", which is one part of the elderly's daily leisure life. Through square dancing, they both meet their friends and exercise. It also adds to their joys of life.

Jiang Yihua: Right. I also often see people in the park sunbathing, chatting and strolling. There are not only a lot of teahouses in Chengdu, but also many cafés. Once, I saw

a lovely café in the street and went inside, where I heard the soft music, smelled the delicious coffee and saw the quiet people. Life was simply beautiful. It was then that I fell in love with Chengdu.

Da Meng: Yes, the cafés are also places people often frequent. You spend one afternoon just like that by going to a café, ordering a cup of coffee, reading a book and getting lost in thought. Or you can go together with friends and chat; time will fly by fast.

Part 2

Jiang Yihua: Da Meng, recently I've been thinking about moving close to school. How should I go about finding a place?

Da Meng: You best go find a housing agency. Their fees are usually one month's rent. They will take you to see an apartment based on your request. Afterwards, you will sign a contract with them and the landlord.

Jiang Yihua: Is it convenient to live near school?

Da Meng: Very much so! There are shopping malls and supermarkets close to school, like Metro, Xidan Shopping Mall and also a lot of small shops. Almost every street in Chengdu has Hongqi convenience stores and Wudongfeng supermarkets, where you can buy food and daily necessities, top up your public transport card, pay electricity, water and gas bills and even buy bus tickets for travel. The school is also close to the subway: at the Culture Palace Station, you can take Line 4 and Line 7. Next to it is the Jinsha bus stop. Transport here is very convenient.

Jiang Yihua: I'll first go to the agency. Another thing, I want to have internet at home. Is that difficult to do?

Da Meng: You can go to China Telecom, China Mobile or other companies. Their staff will go to your apartment and set up an internet connection.

Part 3

Wen Xiaoxi: Yihua, my mom wants to send me something, but I don't know the address of the school, do you?

Jiang Yihua: No. 55 Guanghuacun Street, Qingyang District.

Wen Xiaoxi: Qingyang District? Why is it called like that?

Da Meng: Because Qingyang Gong is in this district.

Jiang Yihua: I heard that Qingyang Gong is a famous Daoist building.

Da Meng: You're right. Inside Qingyang Gong are two black sheep. Legend has it that rubbing these black sheep brings good luck.

Jiang Yihua: I've found that a lot of place names in Chengdu are linked to history.

Da Meng: Correct. Qintai Road and Fuqin District, for example, share a connection with the story about Sima Xiangru and Zhuo Wenjun. Sima Xiangru was a writer from the Han Dynasty and a poor boy. Zhuo Wenjun was the daughter of a wealthy family. Through playing the zither, Sima Xiangru expressed his love towards Zhuo Wenjun. Afterwards, the two of them came to Chengdu in their pursuit of love.

Wen Xiaoxi: If you put it like that, Chengdu is also a city of love.

Da Meng: Well said. There is a place called Hejiang Pavilion. Chengdu's mother rivers are the Fu River and Nan River. After they combine, they are called the Funan river. 1,200 years ago, people erected the Hejiang Pavilion where the two rivers converge. Nowadays, many young people go there to take photos in the morning on the day they're getting married.

Wen Xiaoxi: Two people start to live together, just like how the Fu and Nan rivers come together. How romantic!

Jiang Yihua: I know there's a street called Jin'guanyi Street, because in ancient times, Chengdu was called the "City of the Brocade Officer".

Da Meng: Right, there are many stories about Chengdu's street names.

Wen Xiaoxi: Just imagining the history and stories that once took place in these streets, which are still full of life. It's just so exciting!

词语

合同 **hé tóng** contract	散步 **sàn bù** take a walk; go for a walk; go for a stroll	晒 **shài** bask in (the sunshine)

nèi dì 内地	(China's) inland		yí jū 宜居	livable
zuì jìn 最近	recently; lately; of late		huán 环	ring
gāo jià qiáo 高架桥	viaduct; high trestle bridge; high overpass		guǎng chǎng 广场	(public) square; plaza
xiū xián 休闲	leisure; enjoy leisure		rì cháng 日常	day-to-day; everyday; daily
duàn liàn 锻炼	exercise; work out; practice		zēng jiā 增加	increase; raise; add

lè qù 乐 趣	delight; pleasure; joy
zhōng jiè 中 介	intermediary
gēn jù 根 据	according to; on the basis of; based on
fāng biàn 方 便	convenient
rì yòngpǐn 日 用 品	articles of everyday use
qū 区	area; district; region
jiàn zhù 建 筑	building; construct
wénxué jiā 文 学 家	writer; literati

fā dāi 发 呆	stare blankly; be lost in thought
fáng zū 房 租	rent (for a house, apartment…)
shí pǐn 食 品	food
jì 寄	post; mail; send
tīng shuō 听 说	be told; hear of
Dào jiào 道 教	Daoism; Daoist religion
mō 摸	touch
guān xì 关 系	(often used corre- latively with 没有, 有) relevance; significance; bearing; relation

biǎo dá 表 达	express; convey
làng màn 浪 漫	romantic
xiǎng xiàng 想 象	imagine

xiǎo zi 小 子	guy
huì hé 汇 合	converge; join
qì xī 气 息	flavor; smell; feel

专有名词

1. 红旗连锁 /Hóngqí liánsuǒ / Hongqi convenience store; Hongqi Chain Store

2. 舞东风 /Wǔdōngfēng / Wudongfeng Supermarket

3. 中国电信 /Zhōngguó Diànxìn/ China Telecom

4. 中国移动 /Zhōngguó Yídòng/ China Mobile

5. 青羊宫 / Qīngyáng Gōng / Qingyang Gong; Black Sheep Temple

6. 琴台路 /Qíntái Lù / Qintai Road

7. 抚琴小区 /Fǔqín Xiǎoqū / Fuqin District

8. 合江亭 /Héjiāng Tíng / Hejiang Pavilion

9. 锦官驿街 /Jǐnguān Yìjiē / Jin'guanyi Street

思 考

1. 你觉得成都宜居吗？为什么？

2. 你怎么看在中国城市里流行的广场舞？

3. 你发现成都有趣的街道名了没有？如果有的话，请举例。

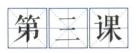 【成都的交通】

Lesson 3 【Transport in Chengdu】

（一）

① 附 近　fùjìn
② 金沙遗址博物馆
　 Jīnshā Yízhǐ Bówùguǎn
③ 博物馆　bówùguǎn
④ 浣花溪公园
　 Huànhuāxī Gōngyuán
⑤ 杜甫草堂
　 Dùfǔ Cǎotáng

文小西：
　明天我们出去玩吧。

江一华：
　好啊，去哪里？就在学校附近吧，不要太远了。

大 萌：
　学校附近有金沙遗址博物馆、杜甫草堂、四川博物院等。你们想去哪里？

文小西：
　我想去逛公园。

大 萌：
　那我们去杜甫草堂吧，旁边还有浣花溪公园。

江一华：
　杜甫草堂有什么历史？

大 萌：

杜甫是唐代伟大的诗人，他在成都住过一段时间，写了很多关于成都的诗，他的家就是现在的草堂。

文 小西：

我们怎么去呢？

大 萌：

可以坐公交车去，打的也可以。你们有公交卡吗？

文 小西：

我有公交卡。

江 一华：

我没有公交卡。要不我们骑共享单车去？

大 萌：

可以，骑车 10 分钟就到了。

文 小西：

我每天都看到校园里、路边停着很多共享单车。我还没有试过呢。

⑥伟 大　wěidà
⑦诗 人　shīrén
⑧共 享　gòngxiǎng
⑨单 车　dānchē
⑩注 册　zhùcè
⑪扫　　sǎo
⑫下 载　xiàzài
⑬二维码　èrwéimǎ
⑭微 信　Wēixin

江一华：

你下载一个共享单车的APP，用你的手机号注册，扫一扫二维码就可以了。不过你得有支付宝或者微信钱包。

文小西：

我的微信钱包里面有钱，那我赶紧下载一个。

（二）

① 滴滴出行　Dīdī Chūxíng
② 支付宝　　Zhīfùbǎo
③ 充　值　　chōngzhí
④ 零　钱　　língqián
⑤ 自　动　　zìdòng
⑥ 售卡机　　shòukǎjī
⑦ 电　子　　diànzǐ

文小西：

共享单车用完了以后，停在路边就可以了，真方便！

江一华：

是啊，现在我都用手机支付。我还用过"滴滴出行"，约了一辆出租车，又快又便宜。

大 萌：

现在地铁站也可以用支付宝或者微信给公交卡充值。

江一华：

我还没有公交卡，在哪里买？怎样充值？

大 萌：

　　成都的公交车都是无人售票，没有零钱的话不太方便，所以最好还是办张公交卡。办卡很简单，在地铁站的自动售卡机就可以买。充值分两种：一种是次卡，另一种是电子钱包。坐公交车可以用次卡，也可以用电子钱包，坐地铁只能用电子钱包。

文 小西：

　　你可以去附近的"红旗连锁"或"舞东风"超市充值。地铁站也可以充值，但只能充电子钱包。

江 一华：

　　那我充个电子钱包，我还没坐过成都的地铁呢。

（三）

大 萌：

　　成都现在已经开通了地铁 1、2、3、4、7、10 号线，到 2020 年年底，还会增加 7 条线。

文 小西：

　　成都的地铁比较新，环境很好，而且不怕堵车，又快又方便。

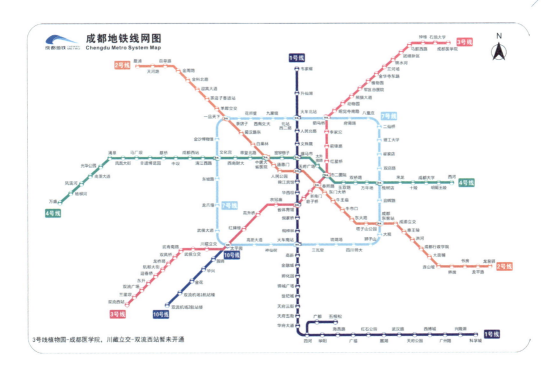

①增 加	zēngjiā	
②堵 车	dǔchē	
③高 铁	gāotiě	
④景 点	jǐngdiǎn	
⑤趟	tàng	
⑥峨眉山	É'méi Shān	
⑦客 运	kèyùn	
⑧中 心	zhōngxīn	
⑨例 如	lìrú	

江一华:

那我下次试试地铁。我坐过高铁去重庆，1个半小时就到了。

大 萌:

现在又新开了成都到西安的高铁，4个小时可以到。你们放假可以去西安玩，西安也有很多景点。

江一华:

买火车票也非常简单，可以在网上买，也可以电话买票，当然，我们也可以去火车站排队买票。

大 萌：

现在还在修成都到贵阳、昆明等地的高铁，成都到外省的高铁会越来越多。

文 小西：

我周末想去趟峨眉山。可以坐高铁去吗？

大 萌：

可以，1个半小时就到了，在成都东站或南站坐高铁。成都有四个火车站，分别是东站、北站、西站和南站。北站是历史最久的火车站，西站最新。

江 一华：

除了坐高铁，还可以坐车去峨眉山吧？

大 萌：

对，去新南门车站坐车。那里有去四川省内各个旅游景点的车。除了新南门汽车站以外，成都市区还有12个客运中心。每个客运中心的车往不同的方向开。例如昭觉寺汽车站主要是往北开的车，比如广元、绵阳、德阳；往东开的车可以在成都汽车总站坐，比如重庆、自贡、泸州、宜宾等；石羊场客运站主要是往西方向的线路，比如雅安、乐山等。

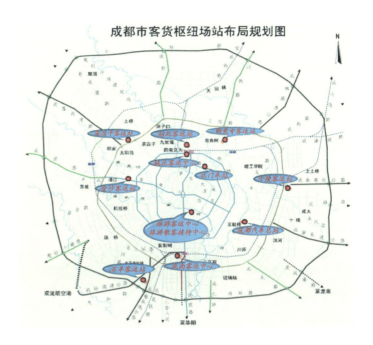

成都市客货枢纽场站布局规划图

江一华：

　　明白了，下次我们要去哪里，先查清楚车站，再去坐车。

大　萌：

　　而且，成都的新机场很快就要建成了。成都将成为中国第三个有两个机场的城市。

文小西：

　　成都的交通真是越来越方便了！

Part 1

Wen Xiaoxi: Let's go out and have some fun tomorrow, how about it?

Jiang Yihua: I'm all for it! Where to? How about close to school? I don't want to go too far away.

Da Meng: Close to our school are, for example, the Jinsha Site Museum, Du Fu Thatched Cottage and the Sichuan Provincial Museum. Where do you want to go?

Wen Xiaoxi: I want to take a walk in a park.

Da Meng: Then let's go to Du Fu Thatched Cottage. The Huan Hua Xi Park is next to it.

Jiang Yihua: What's the history behind Du Fu Thatched Cottage?

Da Meng: Du Fu was a great poet from the Tang Dynasty. He lived in Chengdu for a while and wrote a lot of poems about Chengdu. This thatched cottage used to be his home.

Wen Xiaoxi: So how do we get there?

Da Meng: We can go by bus or call a taxi. Do you have a public transport card?

Wen Xiaoxi: I do.

Jiang Yihua: I don't. How about riding shared bikes?

Da Meng: Sure. It'll take us only 10 minutes to get there.

Wen Xiaoxi: I see a lot of shared bikes parked on the roadside on campus every day. I've never given them a try.

Jiang Yihua: You must have sharing apps first and register with your phone number. Then, scan the QR code on the bike you want to ride and you're good to go. Oh, you also need a Alipay or WeChat wallet.

Wen Xiaoxi: There's some money in my WeChat wallet. I'll go get the app now.

Part 2

Wen Xiaoxi: Once you're done using the bike, you can simply park it on the roadside. How convenient!

Jiang Yihua: It is! I use my phone to pay for everything now. I once also used DiDi to get a ride. It was fast and convenient.

Da Meng: You can also use Alipay or WeChat to top up your public transport card at the subway station.

Jiang Yihua: I don't have a public transport card; where can I buy one? And how do I top it up?

Da Meng: Chengdu's buses run on a self-service ticketing system. If you don't have changes at hand, it's a bit of a hassle, so it's best to have a public transport card. Getting the card is easy: just go to the vending machine in the subway station and buy one. To top it up, you can either buy credits or electronic cash. You can use both credits and electronic cash to pay for a bus ride, but only electronic cash for a subway ride.

Wen Xiaoxi: You can go to a Hongqi convenience store or a Wudongfeng supermarket to top up your card. You can also go to a subway station to top up your card, but only in form of electronic cash.

Jiang Yihua: I'll go top up my electronic cash balance. I've yet to take Chengdu's subway.

Part 3

Da Meng: Chengdu has already opened the subway lines 1, 2, 3, 4, 7 and 10. By the end of 2020, 7 lines will be expanded.

Wen Xiaoxi: Chengdu's subway is relatively new and boasts good travel conditions. You can avoid traffic jams by taking the subway. It's so fast and convenient!

Jiang Yihua: All right, I'll give the subway a try when I have the chance. I took the high-speed train to Chongqing once. I arrived in just one hour and a half.

Da Meng: Another high-speed rail has been opened, from Chengdu to Xi'an, in just 4 hours you'll be in Xi'an. You can go to Xi'an during your vacation; there're lots to see over there.

Jiang Yihua: Buying a train ticket is also really simple. We can get one online, by phone or at the train station, of course.

Da Meng: The high-speed rails between Chengdu and Guiyang, Kunming and other places are also currently under construction. There will be more and more high-speed railway connections from Chengdu to other provinces.

Wen Xiaoxi: I want to go to Mt. Emei this weekend. Can I go there by high-speed train?

Da Meng: You can. It'll take you only one hour and a half. The train departs at Chengdu's East or South railway stations. Chengdu has four railway stations, namely Chengdu East Railway Station, Chengdu North Railway Station, Chengdu West Railway Station and Chengdu South Railway Station. The North station is the oldest, while the West station is the newest.

Jiang Yihua: Other than taking the high-speed rail, I can also take a bus to Mt. Emei, right?

Da Meng: Right, at the Xinnanmen Bus Station. Over there, you can take a bus to Sichuan's various tourist attractions. Apart from Xinnanmen Bus Station, there are 12 passenger transport centers in downtown. The buses of each transport center head to different directions. For example, the bus station at Zhaojue Temple mainly has buses heading northwards to places such as Guangyuan, Mianyang and Deyang. If you want to go eastwards to, for example, Chongqing, Zigong, Luzhou and Yibin, you have to take the buses at the Chengdu Car Terminal. The buses at Shiyang Bus Station mainly head westwards to Ya'an, Leshan and so on.

Jiang Yihua: Got it! Next time we want to go to place, we'll first check what station to go to before we take a bus.

Da Meng: Also, Chengdu's new airport will soon be finished. Chengdu will become China's third city with two airports.

Wen Xiaoxi: Chengdu's transport really is getting better and better!

词 语

| 单 车 | dānchē bicycle | 二 维 码 | èrwéimǎ QR code | 零 钱 | língqián change money |

fù jìn 附 近	nearby; next to; (in the) vicinity	bó wù guǎn 博 物 馆	museum
wěi dà 伟 大	great; important	gòng xiǎng 共 享	share
zhù cè 注 册	register	sǎo 扫	scan
gǎn jǐn 赶 紧	hurriedly; without delay	xià zài 下 载	download
chōng zhí 充 值	recharge; top up; deposit	zì dòng 自 动	automatically

shī rén 诗 人	poet
shòu kǎ jī 售 卡 机	card vending machine
zēng jiā 增 加	increase; raise; add
gāo tiě 高 铁	high-speed railway
tàng 趟	measure word for a round trip
lì rú 例 如	for example; for instance; such as

diàn zǐ 电 子	electronic
dǔ chē 堵 车	traffic jam
jǐng diǎn 景 点	place of interest (tourism); attraction
kè yùn 客 运	passenger transport
rì cháng 日 常	day-to-day; everyday; daily

专 有 名 词

1. 金沙遗址博物馆 / Jīnshā yízhǐ Bówù guǎn / Jinsha Site Museum

2. 杜甫草堂 / Dùfǔ Cǎotáng / Du Fu Thatched Cottage

3. 浣花溪公园　　/ Huànhuāxī Gōng yuán / Huanhuaxi Park

4. 微信　　　　　/ Wēixìn / WeChat

5. 滴滴出行　　　/ Dīdī Chūxíng / DiDi

6. 峨眉山　　　　/ Éméi Shān / Mount Emei

思 考

1. 你在成都市区常常使用哪种交通工具？你觉得怎么样？

2. 你有没有去过成都附近的城市？使用哪种交通工具？说说你的感受。

3. 你对成都的交通有什么意见和建议？

第四课 【成都的外国美食】
Lesson 4 【Chengdu's International Delicacies】

文 小西：

明天我要去见一个从美国来的朋友，我带她去吃点什么呢？

大 萌：

来成都当然要吃川菜。

文 小西：

但我这个朋友不吃辣，有没有什么西餐推荐？

大 萌：

成都除了有很多好吃的川菜馆以外，还有很多外国餐厅。

江 一华：

上次我朋友带我去了桐梓林的红胡子汉堡，那是一家美式餐厅，老板和厨师都是美国人，薯条、汉堡和沙拉都非常地道。旁边还有一家麦可比萨，也是美国人开的，味道很棒。

① 西 餐　xīcān
② 推 荐　tuījiàn
③ 胡 子　húzi
④ 汉 堡　hànbǎo
⑤ 薯 条　shǔtiáo
⑥ 沙 拉　shālā
⑦ 地 道　dìdao
⑧ 比 萨　bǐsà

⑨国　际　guójì
⑩金　融　jīnróng
⑪亚　洲　yàzhōu
⑫美　食　měishí
⑬料　理　liàolǐ
⑭粤　　　yuè
⑮清　淡　qīngdàn
⑯名　单　míngdān

大萌：
太古里和国际金融中心（IFS）也有很多地道的西餐，比如蓝蛙、新元素等，另外也有一些亚洲美食，像泰国菜、日本料理之类的。这些商业中心的中国菜以粤菜为主，口味比较清淡，例如鼎泰丰、翠园。

江一华：
除了市中心，还有哪些地方可以吃到地道的西餐？

大萌：
你可以去桐梓林，因为有很多外国人住在那里，周围就有好吃的西餐厅。现在许多外国人住在世纪城、天鹅湖附近，也很容易找到地道的西餐厅。

文小西：
这样看来，选择还挺多的。

大萌：
这里有一份成都的外国美食名单，我们一起来看看。

Wen Xiaoxi: Tomorrow I'm going to see a friend from the United States. Where should I take her to eat?

Da Meng: Sichuan food, of course. We're in Chengdu after all.

Wen Xiaoxi: But my friend does not eat spicy food. Can you recommend any western-style restaurants?

Da Meng: I can. Apart from Sichuanese restaurants with a wide range of delicious food, Chengdu has also a lot of international restaurants.

Jiang Yihua: My friend took me to Red Beard Burgers at Tongzilin last time. It is an American-style restaurant, both the owner and the chef are American. Their French fries, hamburgers and salads are authentic American food. Next to it is Mike's Pizza Kitchen, which is also operated by an American. Their food is amazing.

Da Meng: At Taikoo Li and the International Financial Square(IFS), you'll find a broad selection of authentic western food, for example, at Blue Frog or Element Fresh, and also Asian delicacies such as Thai and Japanese food. The Chinese food in these commercial centers is mainly Cantonese with light flavors, for instance, Din Tai Fung and Jade Garden.

Jiang Yihua: Aside from the city center, where else can you have some authentic western food?

Da Meng: You can go to Tongzilin, because many people from abroad live there. There are many good western restaurants over there. Many expats live in the Hi-Tech Zone, Century City or near Swan Lake, so it is easy to find authentic western restaurants.

Wen Xiaoxi: Given all that, there is a lot to choose from.

Da Meng: Here is a list of international restaurants in Chengdu. Let's have a look together.

①	意 面	yìmiàn
②	三明治	sān míngzhì
③	猪 排	zhūpái
④	拉 面	lāmiàn
⑤	炸 鸡	zhájī
⑥	冬阴功	dōngyīngōng
⑦	烤	kǎo
⑧	咖 喱	gālí
⑨	河 粉	héfěn
⑩	海 鲜	hǎixiān
⑪	酸 奶	suānnǎi
⑫	蒸	zhēng
⑬	甜品	tiánpǐn
⑭	寿 司	shòusī
⑮	刺 身	cìshēn

餐厅名字	国家(地区)	所在区	地址	电话	特色菜	人均消费(元)
Stay 食库沙拉	欧美	锦江	庆云南街 69 号红星国际 1 幢 2 层 201 号	028-84443858	沙拉	44
RawHeart 生机轻食	欧美	锦江	望平滨河路 34 号	028-84730030	意面、沙拉、三明治	64
Capricciosa 卡布里乔莎意大利料理	意大利	锦江	春熙路东段伊势丹 7 层	028-62499484	意面、比萨、沙拉	96
和幸（双楠伊藤洋华堂 5 楼有分店）	日本	锦江	春熙路大科甲巷 8 号伊势丹 7 楼	028-86662616	炸猪排	74
一风堂拉面	日本	锦江	红星路步行街 3 段 1 号 FS 国际金融中心 LG1 层	028-86586382	拉面、温泉蛋、炸鸡、煎饺	73
尚莲泰国料理	泰国	锦江	远洋太古里东区二层 2320 号	028-81134838	冬阴功、烤猪颈肉、咖喱牛肉	138
Nine road pizzeria 速度披萨	欧美	锦江	红星路步行街 3 段 1 号 IFS 国际金融中心 7 层	028-64861233	比萨	85
兰巴赫西餐•啤酒坊	德国	锦江	锦官驿街 1 号水璟唐文化保护街区 1 栋 7 号	028-65178877	烤脆皮猪肘、巴伐利亚沙拉	118
岘港•越南料理	越南	锦江	大业路 6 号 COSMO 财富中心 2 层	028-86701011	烤鸡、米纸卷、河粉	76
Rico 丽蔻西班牙餐厅	西班牙	武侯	人民南路四段 48 号首座 C 栋 702	15982478776	海鲜饭、羊排、牛排、甜品	145
花图烤肉	韩国	武侯	长荣路泛悦国际外区 2 楼	028-85551574	烤肉	84
沙漠之旅迪拜餐吧	迪拜	武侯	科华中路 150 号金英汇新 7 号 3 幢 301 号	028-67638282	烤肉、酸奶、手抓饭、饼	127
泰喜欢	泰国	武侯	桐梓林东路 10 号	028-64376035	冬阴功、蒸鲈鱼、菠萝炒饭	100
麦可披萨	欧美	武侯	桐梓林路 4 号附 7 号	028-85226453	比萨、烤鸡翅、意面、沙拉	105
红胡子汉堡	欧美	武侯	紫荆东路 29 号	18608031381	薯条、汉堡、沙拉	83
苏坦土耳其餐吧	欧美	武侯	芳华街 25 号附 12	028-85554780	馕、烤鸡、烤肉、土耳其水烟	101
我的四季意大利餐厅	意大利	青羊	二环路西二段光华村街仁和春天百货 C 座 2 楼	028-86156999	比萨、牛排	154

餐厅名字	国家 (地区)	所在 区	地址	电话	特色菜	人均 消费 (元)
仁和春天酒店·春天庭餐厅	欧美	青羊	二环路西二段 19 号仁和春天酒店 3 楼	028-88240901	牛排、鹅肝、甜品	230
彼德西餐厅（多家分店）	墨西哥	青羊	光华村街 50 号大地新光华广场 2 楼	028-87086618	烤薯皮、塔可、沙拉、甜品	86
è pizza 这是比萨	欧美	高新	汇锦城盛邦街 88 号二楼	028-87511171	比萨、烤鸡	75
期会 . 知喜多日本料	日本	高新	天府二街 999 号世豪广场 5 层	028-85979088	刺身、青口、寿司	93
萨波尔西餐	欧美	金牛	二环路北一段 85 号附 30 号	028-85554780	牛排、龙利鱼、意面	101

Restaurant Name	Style	District	Address	Phone	Specialties	Average Price(¥)
Stay	EUR/U.S	Jinjiang	No. 201 , Building 1 Hongxing Internation 2F, No. 69 Qingyun South Street	028-84443858	salads	44
RawHeart	EUR/U.S	Jinjiang	Wangping Binhe Road 34	028-84730030	pasta, salads, sandwiches	64
Capricciosa	I.T	Jinjiang	Isetan 7F, No. 8 Dakejia Alley,East Chunxi Road	028-62499484	pasta, pizza, salads	96
Tonkatsu Wako (with a branch at Shuangnan I to Yokado 5F)	J.P	Jinjiang	Isetan 7F, No. 8 Dakejia Alley, East Chunxi Road	028-86662616	tonkatsu	74
Yifengtang Ramen	J.P	Jinjiang	IFS LG1, No. 1 Hongxing Road 3rd Section	028-86586382	ramen, onsen tamago, karaage,gyoza	73
Lian	Thai	Jinjiang	Sino-Ocean Tai Koo Li East No.2320, F2	028-81134838	tom yum, ko mu yang, beef curry	138
Nine Road Pizzeria	EUR/U.S	Jinjiang	IFS 7F, No. 1 Hongxing Road 3rd Section	028-64861233	pizza	85
LENBACH Restaurant & Bar	D.E	Jinjiang	Shuijingtang Bldg. 1, No. 7, No. 1 Jinguanyi Street	028-65178877	ham hock, Bavarian salads	118

Restaurant Name	Style	District	Address	Phone	Specialties	Average Price (¥)
Pho Viet Keu	V.N	Jinjiang	COSMO Fortune Center F2, No. 6 Daye Road	028-86701011	grilled chicken, rice paper rolls, pho	76
Rico	E.S	Wuhou	Bldg. C, No. 702, No. 48,South Renmin road, Section 4	15982478776	paella, lamp chops, beef chops, desserts	145
Huatu Korean BBQ	K.R	Wuhou	Fanyue International District, Bldg. 2, Changrong Road	028-85551574	BBQ	84
Safari	Dubai	Wuhou	Bldg. 3, No. 301, Jinyinghui No. 7, No. 150,Kehua Middle Road	028-67638282	BBQ, yoghurt, pilaf,flatbread	127
Tai Xihuan	Thai	Wuhou	No. 10, East Tongzilin Road	028-64376035	tom yum,steamed sea bass,pineapple fried rice	100
Mike's Pizza Kitchen	EUR/U.S	Wuhou	No. 4 Ste. 7,Tongzilin Road	028-85226453	pizza, grilled chicken wings, pasta, salads	105
Red Beard Burgers	EUR/U.S	Wuhou	No. 29, East Zijing Road	18608031381	French fries, burgers, salads	83
The Sultan Turkish Restaurant & Bar	EUR/U.S	Wuhou	No. 25, Ste. 12,Fanghua Street	028-85554780	naan, grilled chicken, BBQ, hookah	101
Four Seasons	I.T	Qingyang	Bldg. C, 2F,Ren He Spring Department Store, Guanghuacun Street,West Second Ring Road	028-86156999	pizza, steaks	154
Renhe Spring Restaurant	EUR/U.S	Qingyang	Rehe Spring Hotel 3F, No. 19, Second Section, West Second Ring Road	028-88240901	steaks, foie gras, dessert	230
Peter's Tex-Mex Grill (several branches)	M.X	Qingyang	Dadi Xinguanghua Plaza 2F, No. 50,Guanghuacun Street	028-87086618	baked potato skins, tacos, salads, desserts	98
è pizza	EUR/U.S	Gaoxin	No. 88 ,Shengbang Street, 2F, Huijin City	028-87511171	pizza, grilled chicken	75
Zhi Xi Duo Japanese restaurant	J.P	Gaoxin	World Plaza, 5F, No. 999,Tianfu Second Street	028-85979088	Sashimi, Asian green mussel, sushi	93
Saboer western restaurant	EUR/U.S	Jinniu	No. 85, Ste. 30, Section 1,North Second Ring Road	028-85554780	steaks, sole fish, pasta	101

词 语

	kǎo
烤	roast

		hànbǎo
汉	堡	hamburger

		shǔtiáo
薯	条	French fries

xī cān 西 餐	Western-style food; Western food	tuī jiàn 推 荐	recommend
hú zi 胡 子	beard	bǐ sà 比 萨	pizza
dì dao 地 道	authentic	guó jì 国 际	international
jīn róng 金 融	finance	yà zhōu 亚 洲	Asia
měi shí 美 食	delicacy	liào lǐ 料 理	cook; prepare food

yuè 粤	Cantonese		qīng dàn 清 淡	light (flavor)
míng dān 名 单	list (of names); roster		shā lā 沙 拉	salad
yì miàn 意 面	pasta (Italian noodles)		sān míng zhì 三 明 治	sandwich
zhū pái 猪 排	pork chop		lā miàn 拉 面	ramen (Japane- se); lamian (Chi- nese) (hand-pu- lled noodles)
wēn quán 温 泉	hot spring/well		zhá jī 炸 鸡	fried chicken; karaage (Japa- nese)
dōng yīn gōng 冬 阴 功	tom yum		hé fěn 河 粉	pho (Vietnam- ese); rice noodles
gā lí 咖 喱	curry		suān nǎi 酸 奶	yoghurt
hǎi xiān 海 鲜	seafood		shòu sī 寿 司	sushi

zhēng 蒸	steam
tián pǐn 甜 品	dessert

cì shēn 刺 身	sashimi

思 考

1. 你觉得成都的外国美食怎么样？有什么推荐吗？

2. 你在成都吃过你的家乡菜吗？地道吗？

3. 用汉语介绍一下你的家乡菜和做法。

第五课
Lesson 5

【成都的休闲生活】
【Chengdu's Leisure Life】

①一 般　yìbān
②丰 富　fēngfù
③酒 吧　jiǔbā

（一）

文小西：

成都人周末一般做什么？

大 萌：

本地人的周末生活非常丰富，有的人喜欢喝茶、逛街、看电影，有的人喜欢爬山、运动，有的人喜欢泡酒吧，有的人喜欢打麻将。

江一华：

我发现成都的电影院挺多的。

大 萌：

是的，在市区有很多的电影院和大超市。大家平时就看看电影、逛逛超市，生活很休闲。

文小西：

很多人喜欢打麻将，麻将是什么？怎么玩？

大萌：

　麻将是中国人发明的一种游戏，每副 136 张，它的基本玩法简单，但其中变化很多，玩起来复杂有趣，因此成为中国历史上最吸引人的游戏形式之一。

江一华：

　我早就听说过中国的麻将，也常常看见成都人在茶馆里面边喝茶边打麻将。我也想试试。你可以教我们吗？

④ 发　明　　fāmíng
⑤ 副　　　　fù
⑥ 张　　　　zhāng
⑦ 复　杂　　fùzá
⑧ 基　本　　jīběn
⑨ 吸　引　　xīyǐn
⑩ 形　式　　xíngshì
⑪ 听　说　　tīngshuō
⑫ 不　如　　bùrú
⑬ 建　议　　jiànyì
⑭ 环　境　　huánjìng

大萌：

打麻将挺复杂的，不如我们去一家茶馆，一边喝茶一边学打麻将，怎么样？

江一华：

我们去望江楼公园吧，里面环境不错，打麻将的地方也很多。

（二）

① 打　算　dǎsuàn
② 准　备　zhǔnbèi

大萌：

小西，明天是周末，你打算干什么呢？

文小西：

我和一个新认识的中国朋友约了去逛街。

大萌：

你们去哪里逛街？

文小西：

我们准备去春熙路。

江一华：

周末春熙路的人太多，太挤了吧。

文小西：
人多才热闹呢，大家可以一起玩。

大萌：
太古里和国际金融中心（IFS）很繁华，有很多店可以逛。

江一华：
上次我去太古里的时候经过大慈寺，大慈寺里面很安静，外面很热闹。在繁华里遇到历史，感觉特别棒。

文小西：
对了，一华，那你周末打算干什么？

江一华：
我准备和中国朋友一起去近郊爬山。大萌，你呢？

大萌：
我最近长胖了，我打算去健身房做运动。

文小西：
你不用减肥，熊猫胖胖的才可爱。

③ 热 闹　　rè·nao
④ 繁 华　　fánhuá
⑤ 经 过　　jīngguò
⑥ 大慈寺　　Dàcí Sì
⑦ 安 静　　ānjìng
⑧ 遇 到　　yùdào
⑨ 近 郊　　jìnjiāo
⑩ 健身房　　jiànshēnfáng
⑪ 减 肥　　jiǎn féi
⑫ 熊 猫　　xióngmāo

Part 1

Wen Xiaoxi: What do the people in Chengdu usually do on weekends?

Da Meng: The locals have an incredibly rich weekend: some people like drinking tea, taking stroll in the streets and watching movies; others enjoy climbing and exercising; and there are those who love bar hopping or playing mahjong.

Jiang Yihua: I've found that Chengdu has a lot of movie theaters.

Da Meng: It does, there are lots of movie theaters and big supermarkets in downtown. Everybody usually goes watching movies or window-shopping. Our lifestyle is casual.

Wen Xiaoxi: What is mahjong? How do you play it?

Da Meng: Mahjong is a Chinese invention. A set consists of 136 tiles. It is a complex and thrilling game. Mahjong's basic gameplay is simple, but it has undergone many changes, which have thus made it one of the most appealing forms of entertainment in Chinese history.

Jiang Yihua: I've heard of China's mahjong and I often see Chengdu people in teahouses play mahjong while having tea. I also want to give it a try. Can you teach us?

Da Meng: Mahjong is quite complicated. How about going to a teahouse and learning how to play mahjong over a cup of tea?

Jiang Yihua: I suggest going to Wangjianglou Park. Its environment is good and it has many places for playing mahjong.

Part 2

Da Meng: Xiaoxi, tomorrow's the weekend, any plans?

Wen Xiaoxi: I'm going window-shopping with a newly-acquainted Chinese friend.

Da Meng: Where to?

Wen Xiaoxi: We're going to Chunxi Road.

Jiang Yihua: There are too many people on Chunxi Road on weekends; it'll probably be overcrowded.

Wen Xiaoxi: That just means it's very lively! And we can have a good time together.

Da Meng: Taikoo Li and the IFS are bustling places with many shops to stroll around.

Jiang Yihua: Last time I went to Taikoo Li, I passed through Daci Temple. It's quiet inside the temple and lively outside. It felt amazing to come across a piece of history amidst a bustling environment.

Wen Xiaoxi: By the way, Yihua, what are your weekend plans?

Jiang Yihua: I'm going hiking in the outskirts with my Chinese friends. Da Meng, what about you?

Da Meng: I got fat recently; I plan to go to the gym to work out.

Wen Xiaoxi: There's no need to lose weight. Only fat pandas are cute.

|  jiǔ bā
bar | jiǎn féi
lose weight | xióng māo
panda |

fán huá 繁 华	prosperous, flourishing	yì bān 一 般	usually
fēng fù 丰 富	rich; varied	fā míng 发 明	invent
fù 副	(measure word for a set of sth.)	zhāng 张	(measure word for flat things or flat surfaces); here: tile
fù zá 复 杂	complicated; complex	jī běn 基 本	main; essential; basic; fundamental
xíng shì 形 式	form	tīng shuō 听 说	be told; hear of

bù rú		dǎ suàn	
不 如	how about···	打 算	plan; intend
huán jìng	environment; circumstances; surroundings; conditions	rè nao	lively; bustling
环 境		热 闹	
zhǔn bèi	prepare; get ready; intend; plan	jìn jiāo	suburbs; outskirts
准 备		近 郊	
jīng guò	pass; go through	yù dào	run into; encounter; come across
经 过		遇 到	
ān jìng	quiet; peaceful; silent; calm	jiàn shēn fáng	gym(nasium); fitness center
安 静		健 身 房	

专 有 名 词

大慈寺 / Dàcí Sì / Daci Temple

思 考

1. 你周末一般干什么？

2. 你怎么看成都人喜欢打麻将这件事情？

学 说 成 都 话

成都话与普通话差别不大，具体的区别有：

1. zh、ch、sh、r 说成 z、c、s、r[z]。
2. l 读成 n。
3. ing 和 eng 读成 in、en。
4. 成都话中多"儿"音。

---

1. 行：得行。
2. 好的：要得。
3. 便宜：相因。
4. 什么：啥子？
5. 知道：晓得。
6. 舒服：安逸。

7. 加油：雄起。　　　　8. 怕老婆：炉耳朵。

9. 左转：倒左拐。　　　10. 说的和做的不一样：假打。

11. 没事：不存在。　　　12. 太差了：太撇（pie）了。

13. 聊天：摆龙门阵。　　14. 你骗别人吗：你豁（ho）别个哇？

15. 多少钱：好多钱？　　16. 来不及：搞不赢（gao bu yin）。

17. 做什么：爪子？　　　18. 舒服、好：巴适。

第六课 【在成都工作和生活】
Lesson 6 【Life and Work in Chengdu】

① 强　　qiáng
② 企业　qǐyè
③ 了解　liǎojiě
④ 目前　mùqián
⑤ 活力　huólì
⑥ 风光　fēngguāng

① 杂志　zázhì
② 评　　píng
③ 未来　wèilái
④ 机会　jīhuì
⑤ 教学　jiàoxué
⑥ 外贸　wàimào
⑦ 软件　ruǎnjiàn
⑧ 研发　yánfā
⑨ 比例　bǐlì
⑩ 成立　chénglì
⑪ 创新　chuàngxīn
⑫ 厨师　chúshī
⑬ 叫卖　jiàomài
⑭ 青春　qīngchūn
⑮ 汗水　hànshuǐ
⑯ 一线城市　yīxiàn chéngshì
⑰ 蓉欧快铁　Róng'ōu kuài tiě
⑱ 国家中心城市
　　guójiā zhōngxīn
　　chéngshì
⑲ 最佳表现城市
　　zuìjiā biǎoxiàn
　　chéngshì
⑳ 自贸试验区　zìmào shìyànqū

越来越多的外国人来到成都工作、生活。在成都的世界500强企业有近300家。据了解，目前在成都工作的外国人已经超过3万人。有的人喜欢成都的工作环境和市场活力，有的人喜欢成都良好的居住环境和城市风光。

【一】宜业

成都是中国中心城市之一。《福布斯》杂志把成都评为"未来10年全球发展最快城市"，今天的成都在国内新一线城市里排名第一。成都可以直飞世界100多个国家，也是蓉欧快铁的起点，是离欧洲最近的国家中心城市。

成都被评为中国"最佳表现城市"，有着良好的工作环境。成都自贸试验区也带来了更多的机会，有很好的创业氛围。最近，有不少外国人开始在成都创业。到2017年4月，已经有上千名外国人在成都创业。外国人创业最喜欢开酒吧和饭馆，其次是教学、外贸、软件研发等。前后两者的比例差不多。2017年2月，成都市成立了"外籍人士创新创业之家"。这是一个专门为外国人创业服务的组织。外国厨师把地道的家乡菜带到成都，喜欢音乐的小伙子将广场舞的声音、菜市场的叫卖做成音乐……这些外籍人士把自己的青春和汗水留在了成都的土地上。

【二】宜居

成都因宜居著名，美丽的自然风景、悠闲的生活方式吸引很多人来成都游玩、居住。唐代诗人杜甫的诗句"窗含西岭千秋雪"，写的是离成都约110千米的西岭雪山，也是今天成都人在阳台上就能看到的美景。

成都是一个时尚的城市、温暖的城市。成都人热情幽默、快乐友好。在成都茶馆有9 264家，火锅店5万家，书店1 129家，博物馆数量全国第一。许多外国人把成都看成他们的第二故乡。无论是路边餐馆的炒饭，还是难得的阳光，都是他们生活中不可缺少的一部分。他们也非常享受在成都的生活，有的人在成都找到了自己的另一半，在这里有了温暖的家。

每个人都有自己关于成都的故事，也希望你能够喜欢在这里的每一天，和我们一起分享住在成都的故事。

① 自 然　zìrán
② 公 里　gōnglǐ
③ 阳 台　yángtái
④ 时 尚　shíshàng
⑤ 温 暖　wēnnuǎn
⑥ 热 情　rèqíng
⑦ 幽 默　yōumò
⑧ 友 好　yǒuhǎo
⑨ 故 乡　gùxiāng
⑩ 难 得　nándé
⑪ 缺 少　quēshǎo
⑫ 分 享　fēnxiǎng

More and more people from abroad come to work and live in Chengdu. Of the world's fortune 500 companies, almost 300 have representations in Chengdu. More than 30,000 international workers are known to permanently reside in Chengdu. Some like Chengdu's working conditions and market vitality; others its good living conditions and scenery.

Part 1 【An Environment Favorable for Business 】

Chengdu is one of the National Central Cities. Forbes magazine ranked Chengdu as "the fastest growing city in the world in the next decade". Today, Chengdu ranks first among China's New Tier One Cities. From Chengdu, you can fly to more than 100 countries directly. It is the starting point of the Chengdu-Europe Express Rail and the closest National Central City to Europe.

Chengdu was named China's best performing city and it boasts a good working environment. Chengdu' s Pilot Free Trade Zone also brings more opportunities and provides favorable conditions for startups. Recently, many people from abroad have launched their business in Chengdu. As of April 2017, there are already more than 1,000 foreign entrepreneurs in Chengdu. Their businesses of choice are bars and restaurants, followed by teaching, foreign trade, software R&D and many more. Having said that, the proportion of the former and the latter are more or less the same. In February 2017, Chengdu set up the "home of foreign innovators and entrepreneurs", which is an organization that specifically supports foreign entrepreneurs in their endeavors. Foreign chefs brought their authentic local cuisine to Chengdu and music lovers took the sounds of square dancing and market stallholders who cry their wares and composed them into music. These expatriates have put their blood, sweat and tears in Chengdu.

Part 2 【Livable】

Chengdu is famous for its livability. Its beautiful natural sceneries and laid-back lifestyle draw many to Chengdu for fun and living. Tang poet Du Fu's verse "From my window the snow-crowned western hills are seen" refers to Xiling Snow Mountain, which is 200 km away from Chengdu, but its beauty can even be seen today by Chengdu people on their balconies.

Chengdu gives off vibes both stylish and warm. People here are warm-hearted and humorous, happy and friendly. There are 9,264 teahouses in Chengdu, 50,000 hot pot restaurants, 1,129 book stores and the highest number of museums nationwide. Many expats regard Chengdu as their second hometowns. Be it the fried rice from the roadside restaurant or the rare sunshine, all of this is an indispensable part of their lives. They very much enjoy their lives in Chengdu. Some have even found their other half in Chengdu and have gained a warm home here.

Everyone has his own story about Chengdu. We hope that you are able to enjoy every day here and share with us your story of living in Chengdu.

词 语

杂 志	zá zhì	国 际	guó jì	合 作	hé zuò
	magazine		international		cooperate; collaborate

qiáng 强	strong; powerful	qǐ yè 企 业	enterprise; business
liǎo jiě 了 解	understand	mù qián 目 前	at present; at the moment
huó lì 活 力	vigor; vitality; energy	fēng guāng 风 光	scenery; scene; view; sight
píng 评	choose (by public appraisal)	wèi lái 未 来	next; future; coming
hàn shuǐ 汗 水	sweat	jīng jì 经 济	economy

qǐ diǎn 起 点	starting point
yǒu hǎo 友 好	friendly
jī huì 机 会	chance; opportunity
kē yán 科 研	(scientific) research
chuàng xīn 创 新	innovate
wài mào 外 贸	foreign trade
yán fā 研 发	research and develop
chéng lì 成 立	found; establish; set up

yǒu yì 友 谊	friendship
lǐng shì 领 事	consul
zhí yè 职 业	occupation; profession; professional
zhuān yè 专 业	specialty; specialized field; major; professional
jiào xué 教 学	teach
ruǎn jiàn 软 件	software
bǐ lì 比 例	proportion; scale
chú shī 厨 师	cook; chef

jiào mài 叫 卖		cry one's wares; hawk
gōng lǐ 公 里		kilometer
yōu mò 幽 默		humorous
shù liàng 数 量		number; amount
gù xiāng 故 乡		hometown
fēn xiǎng 分 享		share
quē shǎo 缺 少		lack; be short of

qīng chūn 青 春		youth
zì rán 自 然		nature
yáng tái 阳 台		balcony
shí shàng 时 尚		fashionable
rè qíng 热 情		warm-hearted
nán dé 难 得		hard to come by; rare
wēn nuǎn 温 暖		warmth; warm

专有名词

1. "一带一路" 倡议　　/ "Yídàiyílù"chàngyì / The Belt and Road Initiative

2. 蓉欧快铁　　　　　/ Róng'ōu kuài tiě / Chengdu-Europe Express Rail

3. 西岭雪山　　　　　/ Xīlǐng xuěshān / Xiling Snow Mountain

思考

1. 你为什么来成都生活？

2. 你和成都有怎样的故事？欢迎和大家说说。

参考文献
[References]

[1] 孔子学院总部 / 国家汉办 . 国际汉语教学通用课程大纲 [M]. 北京：北京语言大学出版社，2014.

[2] 北京大学中国语言文学系语言学教研室 . 汉语方音字汇（第二版重排本）[M]. 北京：语文出版社，2003.

[3] 飞乐鸟 . 飞乐鸟的手绘旅行笔记：成都 [M]. 北京：人民邮电出版社，2016.

[4] 四川在线 . 成都高新区外籍人士创新创业之家开门迎客 [EB/OL]. [2017-02-23].http://sichuan.scol.com.cn/fffy/201702/55835601.html.

[5] 大众点评网 . 成都美食 [EB/OL]. http://www.dianping.com/chengdu/food.

[6] 成都市委外宣办 .2017 天府成都形象片（英文版）[EB/OL]. http://v.youku.com/v_show/id_XMzAyOTYwNDc4OA====html?sharefrom=iphone&source=&from=singlemessage&isappinstalled=0.

图书在版编目（CIP）数据

成都印象／西南财经大学 汉语国际推广成都基地著 —成都：西南财经
大学出版社，2019.7
　（走进天府系列教材）
ISBN 987-7-5504-3776-0

　Ⅰ．①成…　Ⅱ．①西…　Ⅲ．①汉语—对外汉语教学—教材②成都—
概况　Ⅳ．①H 195.4②K 927.11
中国版本图书馆 CIP 数据核字（2018）第 241717 号

走进天府系列教材：成都印象·居成都

ZOUJIN TIANFU XILIE JIAOCAI:CHENGDU YINXIANG · JU CHENGDU

西南财经大学　汉语国际推广成都基地　著

策　　　划：王正好　何春梅
责任编辑：李　才
装帧设计：张艳洁
插　　画：辣点设计
责任印制：朱曼丽

出版发行	西南财经大学出版社（四川省成都市光华村街 55 号）
网　　址	http：//www.bookcj.com
电子邮件	bookcj@ foxmail.com
邮政编码	610074
电　　话	028-87353785
照　　排	上海辣点广告设计咨询有限公司
印　　刷	四川新财印务有限公司
成品尺寸	170mm×240mm
印　　张	46.5
字　　数	875 千字
版　　次	2019 年 7 月第 1 版
印　　次	2019 年 7 月第 1 次印刷
印　　数	1-2050 套
书　　号	ISBN 978-7-5504-3776-0
定　　价	198.00 元（套）

1．版权所有，翻印必究。

2．如有印刷、装订等差错，可向本社营销部调换。

3．本书封底无本社数码防伪标识，不得销售。